FRANCES POET

Frances Poet is a Glasgow-based writer. Her work includes *Faith Fall* (Òran Mór and Bristol's Tobacco Factory, 2012) and *What Put the Blood* (Abbey Theatre, 2017). She has also written a number of free adaptations including Strindberg's *Dance of Death* (Citizens Theatre, 2016) and Molière's *The Misanthrope* (Òran Mór, 2014).

Frances's TV and radio work includes *River City* and *The Disappointed*, aired on BBC Radio Scotland in 2015. Her short film, *Spores*, screened at the Edinburgh Film Festival and Bogoshorts Festival, Bogotá, in 2016.

Other Titles in this Series

Frances Poet

ADAM

NICK HERN BOOKS

London

www.nickhernbooks.co.uk

A Nick Hern Book

Adam first published as a paperback original in Great Britain in 2017 by Nick Hern Books Limited, The Glasshouse, 49a Goldhawk Road, London W12 8QP, in association with the National Theatre of Scotland

Adam copyright © 2017 Frances Poet

Frances Poet has asserted her right to be identified as the author of this work

Cover photograph by Andy Bell

Designed and typeset by Nick Hern Books, London
Printed in the UK by Mimeo Ltd, Huntingdon, Cambridgeshire PE29 6XX

A CIP catalogue record for this book is available from the British Library

ISBN 978 1 84842 697 9

**Woodland
CARBON**
www.woodlandcarbon.co.uk
NICK HERN BOOKS
Printed on Carbon Captured paper

Adam was presented by the National Theatre of Scotland and first performed at the Traverse Theatre, Edinburgh, as part of the Made in Scotland Showcase, on 6 August 2017 (previews from 30 July). The cast was as follows:

ADAM/VARIOUS ROLES	Neshla Caplan
ADAM/VARIOUS ROLES	Adam Kashmiry

Featuring a recording of Myriam Acharki as Adam's mother, and additional recorded performances from:

Rylan Gleave
Harry Knights
Juliana Yazbeck
Umar Ahmed
Adam Buksh
Nafee S. Mohammed

Director	Cora Bissett
Composer & Musical Director	Jocelyn Pook
Set & Costume Designer	Emily James
Lighting Designer	Lizzie Powell
Projection Designer	Jack Henry James
Sound Designer	Garry Boyle
Movement Director	Janis Claxton
Voice Coach	Morag Stark
Assistant Director	Rachael Macintyre
Project Manager on The Adam World Choir/ Assistant Producer	Leonie Rae Gasson
Production Manager	Gavin Johnston
Company Stage Manager (Rehearsal Cover)	Alison Brodie
Company Stage Manager	Fiona Findlater
Deputy Stage Manager	Emma Skaer
Assistant Stage Manager	Annie Winton

Lighting Supervisor	Paul Froy
Sound Supervisor	Andy Stuart
Video Supervisor	Ellie Thompson
Stage Supervisor	David Hill
Costume Supervisor	Kylie Langford
Blogger in Residence	Oceana Maund
Cover Photograph	Andy Bell

Adam was conceived for the stage by Cora Bissett

The Company would like to thank

Anna Hodgart, Elly Goodman and Neil Packham, Ben Power, Katrina at LGBT Health, Martha Steed, Douglas Maxwell, George Aza-Selinger, Jamie Christian-Ward, Umama Hamido, Hazel Gray, David Gerber, Urban Outfitters, Julia from New Look (Glasgow), Carol from les100ciels, Melissa Rankin and Rhonda Barclay at The Royal Conservatoire of Scotland.

The Adam World Choir

This performance features videos sent in from members of the Adam World Choir, a global digital community of transgender and non-binary people from the USA to Russia, Denmark to Slovenia, Australia to the Netherlands.

A massive thank-you to every member of the Adam World Choir around the globe who have taken part in the project. Thank you to all the members who sent in their videos and are singing in this production; thanks to the members who wrote down their powerful stories to be shared in a book; thanks to those members who wrote beautiful songs to be featured in the album; thank you to all the amazing artists, programmers and producers who contributed to our digital symposium and the wonderful people who worked front of house; thank you to the brilliant local members who took part in the singing workshop; thank you to the extraordinary performers and artists who presented work as part of the *Home Away* event.

Every member of the Adam World Choir has made this project a glorious celebration of trans and non-binary identities around the globe.

To take part or find out more visit **www.adamworldchoir.net**

[NATIONAL THEATRE OF SCOTLAND]

Artistic Director and Chief Executive: Jackie Wylie
Chair: Seona Reid DBE

The National Theatre of Scotland was established in 2006 and has created over 200 productions. Being a theatre without walls, the Company presents a wide variety of work that ranges from large-scale productions to projects tailored to the smallest performing spaces. In addition to conventional theatres, the Company has performed in airports, schools, tower blocks, community halls, ferries and forests.

The Company has toured extensively across Scotland, the rest of the UK and worldwide. Notable productions include *Black Watch* by Gregory Burke which won four Olivier Awards amongst a multitude of awards, the award-winning landmark historical trilogy *The James Plays* by Rona Munro, a radical reimagining of *Macbeth* starring Alan Cumming, presented in Glasgow and at the Lincoln Center Festival and subsequently, Broadway, New York, and the Olivier Award-winning *Our Ladies of Perpetual Succour*, adapted by Lee Hall from Alan Warner's novel *The Sopranos*.

The National Theatre of Scotland creates much of its work in partnership with theatre-makers, companies, venues and participants across the globe. From extraordinary projects with schools and communities, to the groundbreaking online *5 Minute Theatre* to immersive pieces such as David Greig's *The Strange Undoing of Prudencia Hart*, the National Theatre of Scotland's aspiration is to tell the stories that need to be told and to take work to wherever audiences are to be found.

For the latest information on all our activities, visit us online at nationaltheatrescotland.com

Scottish Government
Riaghaltas na h-Alba
gov.scot

ADAM

For Daisy Hermione

Acknowledgements

Huge thanks to Douglas 'Hero' Maxwell, George Aza-Selinger, Neshla Caplan, Jamie Christian-Ward, Umama Hamido, Harry Knights, David Gerber, Hazel Gray, Davina Shah, Gary McNair, Yvonne Hay, Leigh Kelly, The MacKenzies, Andrew & Maggie Stirk, Janet Stirk and my brilliant gang – Richard, Peter and Elizabeth. Special thanks go to Cora Bissett for bringing me on to her dream team; and, of course, to Adam Kashmiry, who shared his story with such generosity, courage and openness – thank you, Adam.

F.P.

Characters

EGYPTIAN ADAM
GLASGOW ADAM

The two Adams also play:

MARYAM
ADAM AT SIX
ADAM AT NINE
ADOLESCENT ADAM
THE MANAGER
AMIRA
STRANGER
MALAK
HOME OFFICE REPRESENTATIVE
GP
TRANSLATOR
MENTAL-HEALTH NURSE
TONI

This text went to press before the end of rehearsals and so may differ slightly from the play as performed.

Flesh of my Flesh

A room. A screen. A sense of a cramped Glasgow flat but also the inside of a brain.

An Arabic lament plays its painful melody. Lights snap up on EGYPTIAN ADAM *holding a large kitchen knife.* EGYPTIAN ADAM *places it on the floor and then calmly and methodically folds a towel and places it next to the knife.* EGYPTIAN ADAM *then retrieves a mobile phone and places that on the pile.*

EGYPTIAN ADAM *kneels by the pile, unbuttons shirt, lifts out breast and holds the knife to it.*

EGYPTIAN ADAM *presses the blade more and more firmly into the flesh.*

The lament surges.

Blackout.

In the Beginning was the Word

Lights up on GLASGOW ADAM, *who takes in the audience. Regards them in a simple, direct and honest way before beginning.*

GLASGOW ADAM. In Arabic, our words are either masculine or feminine. It's a language which likes things to be one thing or another.

In English, you talk of 'the teacher' and I don't know whether it's a man or a woman – it's irrelevant. Same with 'the student' or 'the friend'.

In Arabic, the word changes – it matters whether my 'friend' is a woman or a man.

In English, when a person says 'I hear you', 'I understand you', 'I love you'. They're not speaking to a woman or a man as they would in Arabic. They are speaking to the soul of the person they are addressing.

I like English. I like the words you have for things.

There's a term – I've forgotten it – for words that have more than one meaning. But the meanings are opposite.

'Sanction' is one. It means 'to permit' but also 'to penalise'. It's two things at once. Opposites that live together within this one little word. And 'screen'. 'To show' but also 'to conceal'.

I love these words. Words are not always black and white. And neither are we.

EGYPTIAN ADAM, *top buttoned-up and restored, joins the scene and defends their mother tongue…*

EGYPTIAN ADAM. We have those words in Arabic too. In Ancient Arabic – Saleem 'One who has been bitten by a snake'. But also 'One who is cured'.

The ADAMS *turn to face each other. Their likeness is striking, in their movements and their clothes. They are two sides of a single coin.*

English isn't so special. It's still 'she' and 'he'. One or the other. Right or wrong. Truth or lie.

English words don't speak to the soul of a person. Who here even knows what a soul is? There are two parts to a soul. Ka and –

GLASGOW ADAM. Ba. What has this got to do with –

EGYPTIAN ADAM. Without the body and its shadow which protects it. Without the name given to a person at their birth, the soul becomes lost.

GLASGOW ADAM. I don't want to talk about Egypt. What my ancestors believed.

EGYPTIAN ADAM. Mama gave me a name.

GLASGOW ADAM. It's too painful to think about Mama.

EGYPTIAN ADAM. Have you forgotten it?

GLASGOW ADAM. It was the wrong name.

EGYPTIAN ADAM. Have you forgotten it?

GLASGOW ADAM. No.

EGYPTIAN ADAM. I can't be explained away with a cute English word. All this begins with Egypt. Where I was born.

GLASGOW ADAM. I was born in Glasgow.

This wounds EGYPTIAN ADAM, *who dons a shawl and becomes* MARYAM.

The Word of Truth

MARYAM. You're lying.

GLASGOW ADAM *reluctantly becomes* ADAM AT SIX.

ADAM AT SIX. No, Mama.

MARYAM. You did it on purpose.

ADAM AT SIX. I didn't.

MARYAM *grabs a child's dress. It is wet with urine so she holds it at arm's length.*

MARYAM. Your auntie made this for you.

ADAM AT SIX. I hate it.

MARYAM. That's because it is ugly. Your auntie has terrible taste. But if she makes you a dress, you wear it.

ADAM AT SIX. I did wear it.

MARYAM. You soiled it. Deliberately.

ADAM AT SIX. No.

MARYAM. What have I taught you? What is our contract? Say
    it for me.

ADAM AT SIX. I promise to be kind.
    I promise not to hurt others.
    I promise always to tell the truth.

MARYAM. And the truth is… you urinated on the dress
    deliberately. I'm taking away your football.

ADAM AT SIX. No, Mama!

MARYAM. It's bad enough that we always have battles over
    what you wear. I'm your mother, if I ask you to wear a dress,
    you wear it.

ADAM AT SIX. I did wear it!

MARYAM. For less than one hour!

ADAM AT SIX. I didn't mean to get it wet.

MARYAM. Then how? How did you manage to wee on this
    dress? Remember your promise. No lies.

ADAM AT SIX. I just copied my cousin. I wanted to go to the
    toilet the way Farouk does. Standing up.

A moment. MARYAM *processes this. Her daughter's
otherness scares her.*

Mama? Are you cross, Mama?

EGYPTIAN ADAM *is back.*

EGYPTIAN ADAM. Born in Glasgow? With no mama? Do
    you want to obliterate everything that came before?

GLASGOW ADAM *doesn't want this.*

Then remember.

Before the Mountains were Born

GLASGOW ADAM *becomes* ADAM AT NINE.

ADAM AT NINE. Mama, you must crouch. You are too tall.

EGYPTIAN ADAM *becomes* MARYAM.

You need to crouch, Mama!

MARYAM *crouches*.

MARYAM. I'm too old for this.

ADAM AT NINE. We must huddle together for we are in grave danger. The orcs are all around.

MARYAM. Orcs in Alexandria, fancy that?

ADAM AT NINE. We are in Middle Earth!

MARYAM. And the orcs are the baddies?

ADAM AT NINE. Sauron is the real baddy. He's evil, always watching and bringing darkness.

MARYAM. Sounds like Mubarak.

ADAM AT NINE. He is a giant eye and if he casts his gaze at you, you can die.

MARYAM. Definitely Mubarak.

ADAM AT NINE. Shhh, they are coming.

MARYAM. 'Oh no, Sam, the orcs are coming.'

ADAM AT NINE. Who said you could be Frodo?

MARYAM. Sorry, I...

ADAM AT NINE. I'm Frodo. He's the main part. You're Sam. Pretend to be short and a bit stupid but very very loyal.

MARYAM. 'Oh no, Frodo, the orcs are coming.'

ADAM AT NINE. You don't sound believable.

MARYAM. Well I'm not as good at pretending as you.

ADAM AT NINE. I'm actually very like Frodo so I don't need to pretend.

I put on the ring and that makes me invisible so I am safe. But hiding like that is dangerous too because it can turn you into Gollum. 'My precious, my precious.' Frodo cannot hide himself for long or he will go mad.

MARYAM. I can't crouch for long or I'll go mad.

ADAM AT NINE. You said you'd play!

MARYAM. Can't you play with your friends?

ADAM AT NINE. Doing our hair and kissing boys' pictures in magazines? I hate it.

MARYAM. You won't always feel that way.

ADAM AT NINE. I'll never fit in with them.

MARYAM. Everything will change when you become a woman, princess. You can't be a hobbit for ever.

MARYAM *becomes* EGYPTIAN ADAM *once more*.

EGYPTIAN ADAM. Lord of the fucking Rings?

GLASGOW ADAM. I love that film.

She Shall Be Called Woman

EGYPTIAN ADAM. I'm playing football in school, running fast as the wind. Faster than them all. Me and the ball, like one, speeding past every last person on the pitch until I tap it into the goal. Like a pro. Goooooooooaaaaaaaal!

I run round the pitch, hi-fives here and there. Sweat forming on my top lip.

Feeling my heart beating hard here.

Boom. Boom. Boom. I am alive.

GLASGOW ADAM. And then…

EGYPTIAN ADAM. I'm in a toilet cubicle and when I wipe myself I see a flash of red on the paper. It's here.

Oestrogen has been swimming through my body. While I played and ran and laughed with my friends it has been stimulating the cells on my chest to grow. Moving my body fat onto my hips, buttocks and thighs. I have a waist, I have breasts and now blood. I feel –

GLASGOW ADAM. Hopeful? Excited?

EGYPTIAN ADAM. Empty.

GLASGOW ADAM. And then the cramps start.

GLASGOW ADAM *curls up in pain.*

EGYPTIAN ADAM *becomes* MARYAM *once more and brings* GLASGOW ADAM (ADOLESCENT ADAM) *a cup of anise tea.*

MARYAM. Anise tea. There's nothing that can't be made better by drinking a cup.

ADOLESCENT ADAM. It smells like Baba's socks.

MARYAM. Drink it. Best not to think of your father's socks.

ADOLESCENT ADAM *sips at the tea.*

Today is a happy day.

ADOLESCENT ADAM. Is it?

MARYAM. My little princess is a woman.

ADOLESCENT ADAM *doesn't like this, pushes the tea away.*

ADOLESCENT ADAM. This is too hot.

MARYAM. You don't feel it yet?

ADOLESCENT ADAM *gives a shake of the head.*

Let me help you.

MARYAM *takes out a vanity case and puts make-up and feminine clothes on* ADOLESCENT ADAM. *When she is finished,* MARYAM *holds a mirror to* ADOLESCENT ADAM.

Well, what do you think?

ADOLESCENT ADAM *doesn't answer. A moment.*

Garments of Skin

EGYPTIAN ADAM *addresses the audience again.*

EGYPTIAN ADAM. I am in a room full of women's clothes. Rails of different fabrics and colours. Mannequins wearing the latest fashions. Hip music blasting into the street to entice in potential shoppers. Not me. I work here now. I am a 'visual merchandiser'.

The other staff have an easy way of talking to shoppers, charming and effortless. I watch them and try to be invisible. A pretty woman who smells sweet like Mama's Harisa passes me a dress she wants to try on. I walk her to the dressing room, hang up the dress and return to being invisible.

GLASGOW ADAM *becomes* THE MANAGER.

THE MANAGER. Hey? What are you doing? You don't just leave the customer in there.

EGYPTIAN ADAM. Sorry. I just did it how I saw him do it.

THE MANAGER. Different for guys. Women don't want them hanging round the cubicle. You need to stay, offer advice, pick out alternatives. Go on.

EGYPTIAN ADAM. What advice should I give?

THE MANAGER. I don't know. You're the woman. Tell her what looks good. And smile more – you look like thunder.

EGYPTIAN ADAM *tries on a smile.*

EGYPTIAN ADAM (*to the imagined woman, in the dressing room*). Hello. How is it? Would you like me to look? Do you like the… er, fabric? The way it moves? Is the colour right?

(*To the audience.*) The sweet-smelling woman comes out in the dress. She worries it is too tight here. Is it too short? Can I see her knickers when she bends over?

I don't know this game but I learn fast.

GLASGOW ADAM. I learn how women wear clothes and I use it to better pass as one myself. I watch the way they move, talk and laugh and teach myself how.

GLASGOW ADAM *manipulates* EGYPTIAN ADAM *like a mannequin.*

Slow down. That's too fast. Don't walk like a soldier. Relax. Lower the shoulders. Softer, slower, smoother. Arch the back. Walk with the hips. Take it easy.

Use the hands when talking. Not like that. Not like a gangster. Hold the hand to the face. But don't speak – the voice is too flat and coarse. It needs to be softer, higher, an occasional squeal of excitement.

GLASGOW ADAM *attempts a squeal of laughter.*

EGYPTIAN ADAM. That is your best squeal? It sounds like a growl.

GLASGOW ADAM. Maybe that is why I am taken off the shop floor and put in charge of dressing the mannequins.

EGYPTIAN ADAM. And it's there that I meet…

GLASGOW ADAM. There's no need to tell them about her.

EGYPTIAN ADAM. It's there that I meet…

Visible and Invisible

EGYPTIAN ADAM *pulls on a hijab and becomes* AMIRA. *She drags a female mannequin into the centre of the room.*

AMIRA. No, no, no, you're making it up.

GLASGOW ADAM (*to the audience*). Amira.

AMIRA. Samantha from Sex and the City?

GLASGOW ADAM. It's true.

AMIRA. She's Egyptian?

GLASGOW ADAM. She's hiding in a pyramid because she doesn't want to marry the man her mother has chosen for her and the gods save her.

AMIRA. And turn her into a mannequin?

GLASGOW ADAM. Exactly.

AMIRA. It sounds terrible.

GLASGOW ADAM. You would love it. It is an excellent film.

(*Pulling at the dress.*) It needs to come back this way.

AMIRA. It is snagging here on her tits.

GLASGOW ADAM. It will always snag – her nipples are like two metal doorbells.

AMIRA. They're perfect. Don't tell me you wouldn't want tits like hers.

GLASGOW ADAM *is uncomfortable.*

GLASGOW ADAM. You sound like The Manager…

AMIRA. 'Virginity is curable.'

GLASGOW ADAM. Did he say that? Gross.

AMIRA. I called him on it once. The way he talks about women.

GLASGOW ADAM. What did he say?

AMIRA. 'Sorry, I'm a bit deaf in this ear. Had a hot bitch moaning in it all night.'

GLASGOW ADAM. He told me to wear more make-up –
touched me here and here.

AMIRA. He's a fucking sleazebag. Ignore him – you're perfect.

Embarrassed, GLASGOW ADAM *pulls over a male
mannequin.*

GLASGOW ADAM. Just this one left to do.

AMIRA. Mr No-Cock. He won't take long.

GLASGOW ADAM *looks at* AMIRA.

What?

GLASGOW ADAM. Nothing. Just. Talking to you is… like
breathing in fresh air.

I feel like I could tell you stuff.

AMIRA. You could tell me anything.

A moment. AMIRA *leans in and kisses* GLASGOW ADAM,
who breaks away.

GLASGOW ADAM. You shouldn't do that.

AMIRA. Why?

GLASGOW ADAM. Somebody could see us.

AMIRA. Is that what's stopping you?

Nobody comes down here.

AMIRA *kisses* GLASGOW ADAM *again, who kisses her
back. They stop and sit for a moment.* GLASGOW ADAM
starts laughing a little.

GLASGOW ADAM. That was nice.

AMIRA. I know.

GLASGOW ADAM. That was really nice.

GLASGOW ADAM *giggles.*

AMIRA. Was that what you were going to tell me?

GLASGOW ADAM. No. I mean… partly maybe.

AMIRA. What then?

GLASGOW ADAM. Forget it.

AMIRA. Tell me.

GLASGOW ADAM. It'll sound strange.

AMIRA. I just kissed you, didn't I? I'm okay with strange.

GLASGOW ADAM. Okay. Agghhh. Um, okay. You ever seen the film, Alien?

AMIRA. Not another film!

GLASGOW ADAM. There is an alien that lives inside and bursts out and.

AMIRA. Yes.

GLASGOW ADAM. No. That's not a good comparison. I sometimes feel like I… This is going to sound so weird but. Like I'd be a better boy than a girl.

AMIRA. That doesn't sound weird.

GLASGOW ADAM. It doesn't?

AMIRA. I've felt like that.

GLASGOW ADAM. Really?

AMIRA. We're the same, you and me.

GLASGOW ADAM. You think so?

AMIRA. Girls like us, we should be boys. Staying out late, going wherever we want. Wearing whatever we want. Talking to whoever we want. Kissing whoever the fuck we want.

AMIRA *leans in to kiss* GLASGOW ADAM *who leans in to her.*

Who wouldn't want to be a boy when they have it so good?

AMIRA *kisses* GLASGOW ADAM, *who breaks away.*

What's wrong?

GLASGOW ADAM. Nothing.

(*To the audience*.) To screen – to reveal and to conceal. Both at once.

They Realised They Were Naked

GLASGOW ADAM. I'm in the storeroom with Amira again. After weeks of secret kissing. It's late. There's no window and the yellow electric lights buzz down on us. It's stuffy and oppressive but, with the door locked, we're safe here.

GLASGOW ADAM *is dressing a male mannequin. AMIRA tries to get* GLASGOW ADAM*'s attention, being playful and provocative with the sale clothes. She undresses the female mannequin in the style of a striptease.* GLASGOW ADAM *joins in with the male mannequin. It is light-hearted and sexy. They kiss.*

Is the door locked?

AMIRA. Relax.

GLASGOW ADAM *looks back towards the door to check they are safe.*

Stop looking at the door. Nobody's here but us.

GLASGOW ADAM. We still have lots to do.

AMIRA. There's time.

GLASGOW ADAM *caresses* AMIRA*'s face. In return,* AMIRA *explores* GLASGOW ADAM*'s face with her hands. It is tender and intimate. She moves her hands down to* GLASGOW ADAM*'s chest.* GLASGOW ADAM *catches her hands aggressively.*

GLASGOW ADAM. Don't touch me there. I'll cut your hands.

AMIRA *retreats, dressing one of the mannequins.*

Sorry. I'm sorry. Amira?

AMIRA. You're so conservative.

GLASGOW ADAM. What?

AMIRA. Just because we can't kiss out on the street doesn't
mean they are right. If we were born in a different place and
time, we could get married. Even here in Egypt, in Ancient
times we could be married. You're ashamed of what you are.

GLASGOW ADAM. What am I?

AMIRA. You're the one who likes words. You choose. In the
West, they say 'lesbian'. We're lesbians.

GLASGOW ADAM. That's not what I am.

AMIRA. You prefer 'Shezoz'? What we do is not from
'abnormality'. I see the words on my brother's newspaper –
I should believe we are part of an 'emergency disease'? We
are two girls who love each other, not a threat to the Nation
of Egypt.

GLASGOW ADAM (*whispered*). I'm not a girl.

AMIRA *laughs, stops. Laughs again.*

AMIRA. You look like a girl to me.

GLASGOW ADAM *retreats.*

(*As a flirtation.*) I like how you look. I like your curves.
I like your skin. I like how it feels when we kiss. I like your
softness against my face, your tongue in my mouth.

AMIRA *is close to* GLASGOW ADAM *now. They kiss.*
GLASGOW ADAM *steps out of the kiss.* AMIRA *remains in
it, frozen like a mannequin.*

GLASGOW ADAM (*to the audience*). It's because she tastes so
good. That's why I don't hear his footsteps. Why I don't hear
the door pushed open. Why I don't see him. The Manager.
Standing there. His shirt undone a button too far, his chest
hair damp with sweat, rising and falling as he catches his
breath. And on his face... a smile. He's enjoying what he's
watching. He knows the power it will give him.

GLASGOW ADAM *steps back into the kiss*. AMIRA, *seeing the imagined form of* THE MANAGER, *pulls away in fright. She points towards* GLASGOW ADAM.

AMIRA. She kissed me. I... I'm not.

(*To* GLASGOW ADAM.) You disgust me.

AMIRA *runs away and becomes* EGYPTIAN ADAM *once more*.

GLASGOW ADAM. Amira?

EGYPTIAN ADAM. Just me and The Manager now. Nothing spoken. He takes a step forward and I flinch. He laughs.

GLASGOW ADAM *becomes* THE MANAGER.

THE MANAGER. I'm not going to hurt you.

Give me your hand.

EGYPTIAN ADAM *tentatively holds out a hand.*
THE MANAGER *takes it and rubs it against himself.*
EGYPTIAN ADAM *pulls away.*

I'm helping you. You won't want girls when you've felt what I can give you.

EGYPTIAN ADAM *goes to slap him.* THE MANAGER *catches* EGYPTIAN ADAM*'s arm.*

You need to be careful. The police won't lock you up if they arrest you. Men, they lock up. Women, they cure. You want a gang of four or five policemen to cure you, or me? Who do you think will be more gentle?

THE MANAGER *pulls* EGYPTIAN ADAM *towards him and gives a rough kiss.*

Good girl. We can have some fun, you and me.

THE MANAGER *becomes* GLASGOW ADAM *once again. Disgusted, wipes away the make-up* MARYAM *applied.*

Cursed is the Ground

EGYPTIAN ADAM *gasps as if waking from a dream.*

EGYPTIAN ADAM. It is the middle of the night. In my dream, I am trying to run after Amira. But when I look down, I have no legs. Instead I have a giant scaly tail of a fish. I look like the pictures on the adverts telling people to visit Alexandria – The Mermaid of the Mediterranean.

I get up to wash the sweat from my face. I have legs again but the face that looks back at me in the mirror is wrong. I scrape back my hair and put on a baseball cap. I pull on my father's jacket. I roll up a sock and place it in my trousers and I look long and hard.

It's hard to get enough air to breathe when I first step out onto the street. It's so dark, I've no shadow to protect me. What if somebody sees me?

What if I am stopped?

I need a name.

I am… Peter Parker. I am Bruce Wayne. I am Harvey Dent.

'Hi, I'm Harvey.'

My ancestors feared the two parts of the soul losing its body, its shadow, its name but my heart is soaring like Ba, the human-headed bird of my soul.

I pass a group of guys. They smell of booze and sweat. I speed up to pass them but one of them shouts at me.

GLASGOW ADAM *becomes the* STRANGER.

STRANGER. Oi!

EGYPTIAN ADAM. My heart is in my throat. I keep walking. These men, if they realised what I am, could kill me.

STRANGER. Oi! You.

EGYPTIAN ADAM. I turn to look.

STRANGER. You deaf or what?

EGYPTIAN ADAM. Sorry I didn't hear… (*Adopting a persona.*) I've had a hot bitch moaning in my ear all night.

The STRANGER *is surprised by this, laughs.*

They cheer at me. They like Harvey. Harvey likes them.

Amira has changed me. The truth of who I am is bubbling up in me like a volcano. The world I live in is dangerous but so am I.

Music blasts out, a dangerous and loud beat. It's party time for an emboldened EGYPTIAN ADAM. *This feels great. Friends everywhere – hi-fives, handshakes, man-hugs. Fitting in with people through mutual obliteration. But things begin to go bad. Paranoia creeps in for* EGYPTIAN ADAM. *The friends stop being friends. Their contact becomes more physical.* EGYPTIAN ADAM *is getting bumped up against, groped. People don't like that they can't place* EGYPTIAN ADAM's *gender. We might even hear 'Shezoz' , 'Ya wad ya bet', 'Hey boy, girl', 'It's got breasts', 'Has it got a pussy?' It's starting to feel really threatening.* EGYPTIAN ADAM *stumbles to the floor is dragged to a dark corner. 'I found a pussy', 'It's a woman', 'Let me see', 'Is it wet?'*

Woe to Those Who Quarrel with Their Maker

GLASGOW ADAM *turns off the music and becomes* MALAK, *Adam's dad.* EGYPTIAN ADAM, *startled and broken, stumbles into him.*

MALAK. Did you lose your key?

EGYPTIAN ADAM. I'll pay for a new one.

MALAK *looks at* EGYPTIAN ADAM, *who feels self-conscious, removes cap and anything obviously masculine.*

Go back to bed, Baba.

MALAK. I wasn't in bed. I couldn't sleep.

EGYPTIAN ADAM. 'Cause of me?

MALAK. Maybe. Mostly 'cause your mama is talking in her sleep.

EGYPTIAN ADAM. So you tiptoed out of the room? Mustn't disturb Mama, even if she disturbs you.

MALAK. She needs her sleep.

EGYPTIAN ADAM. And you? What do you need? Creeping around in the middle of the night in your slippers and gown, like an old woman.

MALAK. I need you to calm down.

EGYPTIAN ADAM. Go on then. Tell me how I dishonour you. Your daughter out on the street at this time. Tell me how dangerous it is.

MALAK. I'll make you a cup of anise tea.

EGYPTIAN ADAM. Fucking tea. Doesn't work.

MALAK. I think *you* need some sleep.

EGYPTIAN ADAM. Shout at me!

Forbid me from going out. Teach me how to behave like a daughter should.

MALAK. There's no need for shouting.

EGYPTIAN ADAM. Protect me! Isn't that what a father's supposed to do?

EGYPTIAN ADAM breaks down a little here, vulnerable and distressed from the sexual assault so recently experienced.

It's your job to keep me safe!

MALAK. Shhhh, your mama's sleeping.

This disregard for the pain in front of him, and preoccupation with Mama, wounds EGYPTIAN ADAM deeply.

EGYPTIAN ADAM. You aren't a man. You're weak like a woman. I don't dishonour you. You dishonour me.

EGYPTIAN ADAM spits in MALAK's face, who impulsively strikes back with a slap. A moment. Both shocked. EGYPTIAN ADAM recovers first and starts a slow clap. MALAK shakes his head and goes to leave. He stops and says quietly.

MALAK. I don't think you should buy a new key.

EGYPTIAN ADAM realises the line has been crossed.

MALAK becomes GLASGOW ADAM once more.

I was Afraid and I Hid

GLASGOW ADAM. I am sleeping on the floor of a run-down apartment in Bakos. Not a part of Alexandria they write about in the guidebooks. 'Visitors mustn't miss the exotic sights of this charming apartment building – entertainment includes late-night raids on drug-dealing neighbours, murder bingo and frequent visits from local celebrity, Mr Rat, who will scratch his autograph into your skin on request.'

I am here because I am hiding. From Amira's brother. I don't know what she told him but his friends delivered the message that I disgust and frighten him. He is frightened, not of me, but of what he will do if he sees me. He doesn't want to be a murderer. That's something I suppose.

EGYPTIAN ADAM *becomes* MARYAM.

MARYAM. Tell me you're not sleeping here, princess?

GLASGOW ADAM. Just for a couple of nights.

MARYAM. It's either very dirty or it's a new style of decoration I've not read about.

GLASGOW ADAM. It's not so bad.

MARYAM. It's not so bad for an animal. No human could call this place home.

GLASGOW ADAM. Where should I call home? Will Baba let me come home?

MARYAM *lowers her eyes and does not answer.*

But if you asked him… He'd do anything for you.

MARYAM. I have food for you.

GLASGOW ADAM. Did you bring me some baba ganoush?

MARYAM. No. Some of my kebda eskandarani.

GLASGOW ADAM. Ah, Mama!

MARYAM. It's good for your skin and it'll make your hair glossy.

GLASGOW ADAM. Liver makes me gag.

MARYAM. Not the way I cook it.

GLASGOW ADAM. Especially the way you cook it.

MARYAM. Eat a mouthful for your mama. Your father always says it puts hairs on his chest.

GLASGOW ADAM. If it'll put hairs on my chest…

MARYAM (*with an edge*). If a woman sees a hair on her chest, she should pluck it out.

Same goes for the chin. I've taught you that.

(*Softer now.*) I wish somebody would tell your auntie…

GLASGOW ADAM *reluctantly opens the food and takes a mouthful.*

It's good? See. You're a good girl.

GLASGOW ADAM. It's not so bad. If you swallow without letting it touch your tongue.

MARYAM (*teasing*). How did I raise such a rude daughter?

A beat. GLASGOW ADAM *wants to confide in her.*

GLASGOW ADAM. I'm sorry that I'm not what you raised me to be.

MARYAM. Don't be silly. You're my perfect princess.

GLASGOW ADAM. But Mama –

MARYAM *doesn't want to hear.*

MARYAM. Your cousin has had a little boy.

GLASGOW ADAM. That's great news. I want to meet him. I'll tickle his little toes.

MARYAM. I don't think Farouk will allow it.

GLASGOW ADAM. He doesn't approve of tickling?

MARYAM. He's very angry about the rift between you and your father.

GLASGOW ADAM. *Farouk* is angry?

What about you? You've said nothing but if you wanted me home…

MARYAM. The baby's very ugly. I hold him and kiss him but I find it hard to look at him. Very fat and very ugly. But your auntie married Asif so I don't think she minds ugly things –

GLASGOW ADAM. Inside me, Mama. Inside me is –

MARYAM. Is there a window in this apartment that isn't cracked? Every pane. Like somebody has declared war on windows.

GLASGOW ADAM. Mama, please, I have something I need to say.

MARYAM (*very intense*). No! I don't want those words.

GLASGOW ADAM. But I need to tell you the truth of –

MARYAM. Just lie! Just… lie, princess.

The Tree of Knowledge

The two ADAMS *sit, despondent.*

GLASGOW ADAM. If I don't say it out loud, I will burst.

EGYPTIAN ADAM. Write it.

GLASGOW ADAM. On paper? Somebody will see.

EGYPTIAN ADAM. On the computer. Type it as a question.

GLASGOW ADAM. And press send? Are you mad? I might as well stand at the window and shout it out. People have been arrested for less.

EGYPTIAN ADAM. The woman who lent me this laptop described the internet as a brain. To type a question is just to have a thought, an electric spark in a global brain of ideas.

GLASGOW ADAM. Can I be punished for a thought?

EGYPTIAN ADAM *opens the laptop.*

GLASGOW ADAM *types a question, which appears on the screens.*

CAN THE SOUL OF A MAN BE TRAPPED IN A WOMAN?

The question sits for a moment.

The TV screens begin to flicker, sounds of static and distorted voices surge. Faces flicker on to the screen. Words become discernible.

Here are the faces of people who dare to share themselves on the internet. They are experience, they are knowledge, they are the understanding ADAM *has never had.*

Fragments of testimony from trans people across the world morph into something musical. A global choir of experience and knowledge. It is beautiful but there is disharmony too. The many voices are overwhelming.

GLASGOW ADAM *is transfixed.*

I. Am. Real.

Fearfully and Wonderfully Made

GLASGOW ADAM. It is 2010. I am in Glasgow. I am an asylum seeker! I have been placed in this room. I live, eat and sleep here. The single window is painted shut and the dirty sky I see through it matches the colour of the walls. I have a fridge, a microwave, a toilet and sink, a bed that hurts to sleep on so I choose the floor and a TV on which only Channel 5 works.

It doesn't matter. I am here.

During the following dialogue, GLASGOW ADAM *binds* EGYPTIAN ADAM's *chest. It is very tight and very uncomfortable for* EGYPTIAN ADAM.

I shave my head, I wear men's clothes. I say goodbye to my birth name.

I have a new name.

GLASGOW ADAM *is finished, looks at* EGYPTIAN ADAM *and nods with satisfaction.*

Adam.

EGYPTIAN ADAM. The First Man?

GLASGOW ADAM. That's not why I chose it.

EGYPTIAN ADAM. Cast out of heaven for plucking fruit from the Tree of Knowledge.

GLASGOW ADAM. Knowledge was worth it. Egypt wasn't heaven.

EGYPTIAN ADAM. Do you know how they punished Ancient Egyptians for sins against the gods?

GLASGOW ADAM. Played them Justin Bieber over and over? 'Baby, baby, baby'–

EGYPTIAN ADAM. Banishment. Cut off from the protection and resources of your own people, forced to seek kindness from people who are not your own. Most would die. This room, this is exile.

GLASGOW ADAM. Exile is nothing new. I've lived it my whole life.

Here it is safe to be what I really am.

EGYPTIAN ADAM. What is that?

GLASGOW ADAM. A transgender.

EGYPTIAN ADAM. Mama gave me one of those when I was six.

GLASGOW ADAM. That is a Transformer. Stop trying to provoke me. I am trans. Is that better?

EGYPTIAN ADAM. Egypt is trans. Transcontinental. It is Asia and Africa. Egypt was home to the first trans man. A pharaoh – Hatshepsut. Born a woman but ruled with a beard and the headdress of a king. I see no pharaohs here. Why am I?

GLASGOW ADAM. Because it is meant to be. I'm on a quest, like Frodo, carrying the ring to the Crack of Doom.

EGYPTIAN ADAM. AKA Glasgow.

A reproving look from GLASGOW ADAM.

GLASGOW ADAM. When I sold all that I had and bought the plane ticket to Britain, I did not know it but the highest court in this land was making a decision. That nobody can be forced to return to a place where the only way they can be safe is to hide who they are. The same moment I decided that hiding would destroy me just as it does Frodo when he wears the ring, this country made the same decision.

EGYPTIAN ADAM. Enough already with the Lord of the fucking Rings.

The anger drains out of EGYPTIAN ADAM *for a moment.*

I miss home. I want to go home.

GLASGOW ADAM. I will go home. Tell me it is safe for me in Egypt and I will go home.

EGYPTIAN ADAM *can't.*

(*Tender.*) Here I can do what Mama raised me to do. Tell the truth and show the world who I am.

I am Adam.

EGYPTIAN ADAM *becomes* HOME OFFICE REPRESENTATIVE.

HOME OFFICE REPRESENTATIVE. Were you living as a man in Egypt, Miss Kashmiry?

GLASGOW ADAM. Um, no, I. My name is Adam, please call me Adam.

HOME OFFICE REPRESENTATIVE. Was Adam a name you went by in Egypt?

GLASGOW ADAM *gives a shake of the head.*

GLASGOW ADAM. I tried other names. In my head, many names.

HOME OFFICE REPRESENTATIVE. Did you ever explain your condition to a doctor in Egypt?

Another shake of the head.

Who knew you were transgender, Miss Kashmiry?

GLASGOW ADAM. It's Adam.

HOME OFFICE REPRESENTATIVE. I'll repeat the question. Who knew you were transgender in Egypt?

GLASGOW ADAM. Nobody.

HOME OFFICE REPRESENTATIVE. Let me rephrase. How many friends knew you were transgender?

GLASGOW ADAM. None.

HOME OFFICE REPRESENTATIVE. None?

GLASGOW ADAM *nods.*

And now? Who in your family knows you are transgender, Miss Kashmiry?

GLASGOW ADAM. Nobody.

HOME OFFICE REPRESENTATIVE. Not even your own mother?

GLASGOW ADAM. When my mother tells me she loves me she says 'ana bahibbik'. I love you – a girl – her daughter. She can never love me as a boy, a son – ana bahibbak.

Can you hear it? BahibbIK for a girl, bahibbAKfor a boy. I cannot be loved in Arabic.

HOME OFFICE REPRESENTATIVE. I understand you entered the UK on a holiday visa, Miss Kashmiry – is that correct?

GLASGOW ADAM. I didn't know you could seek asylum in your own country.

HOME OFFICE REPRESENTATIVE. Your application stated that you were from a wealthy family, visiting family friends in the UK and that you intended to return home. You even bought a return plane ticket, is that correct?

GLASGOW ADAM. If I had known I could travel to Cairo and claim asylum, I would have –

HOME OFFICE REPRESENTATIVE. How much of the statement that you signed on that visa was correct?

GLASGOW ADAM. I lied on the forms so I could stop being a liar.

HOME OFFICE REPRESENTATIVE. Please answer the question.

GLASGOW ADAM. I was homeless in Egypt. I had no job. And no chance of getting one without presenting myself in the expected way for a woman.

HOME OFFICE REPRESENTATIVE. Could it be said, therefore, that your reasons for wanting to live in the UK relate to your employment prospects, Miss Kashmiry?

GLASGOW ADAM. No!

Madam I'm Adam!

It's a palindrome. The same forwards as it is backwards.
Madam I'm Adam.

Sorry, I…

HOME OFFICE REPRESENTATIVE *makes notes.*

What are you writing?

EGYPTIAN ADAM *thrusts the* HOME OFFICE
REPRESENTATIVE*'s notes at* GLASGOW ADAM.

EGYPTIAN ADAM. The credibility of your claim has been
undermined by fundamental discrepancies in your testimony.
The Secretary of State does not believe your claim to be
a transgender man.

GLASGOW ADAM *is devastated.*

What now? I appeal and what? Wait? I'm not allowed to
work. Thirty-five pounds is not enough to live on. I have no
debit card. The only ID I'm given has my birth name on it
and states I'm a woman.

GLASGOW ADAM. 'To sanction – to permit but also to
penalise.'

I've escaped Egypt for another prison.

*The stage becomes the claustrophobic Glasgow room which
is also* ADAM*'s brain. Things will start to distort from here.
Time passes in a fluid blur. The passing of the days may be
charted 1, 9, 78, 113… The* ADAMS *are prowling, pacing
the space, trapped. CCTV footage, lots of different angles, of*
ADAM *living in the flat, eating, sleeping, watching TV.*

*The soundscape is of bad daytime TV and taps turning on
and off, the microwave pinging.*

It is oppressive.

EGYPTIAN ADAM. I can't breathe in this binding.

GLASGOW ADAM. I need to prove I am a man.

EGYPTIAN ADAM. My ribs are bending into my lungs. If
I cough, they will tear.

GLASGOW ADAM. I need testosterone.

GP (EGYPTIAN ADAM). You know I can't prescribe that for you, Miss Kashmiry.

GLASGOW ADAM. Adam, please.

GP. You will need to speak again with the consultant psychiatrist at the gender clinic.

GLASGOW ADAM. I have. She will not prescribe the hormone therapy until I am granted asylum. They will not grant me asylum because I have not begun the hormone therapy.

GP. I'm sorry, there's nothing I can do.

GLASGOW ADAM *hardens*.

GLASGOW ADAM. On one of the websites I have found, there is a GP 'shit list'. For trans people who are treated badly...

GP. Are you implying I'm on that list, Miss Kashmiry?

EGYPTIAN ADAM *once more*.

EGYPTIAN ADAM. I promise to be kind.
I promise not to hurt others.
I promise always to tell the truth.

Still in the imagined scene with the GP, GLASGOW ADAM*'s aggression melts away.*

GLASGOW ADAM. No. No. I'm just asking you, please, to help me.

GP. Good luck with your asylum appeal, Miss Kashmiry. Please can you close the door on your way out.

GLASGOW ADAM. Help me, please.

The GP *has gone.* EGYPTIAN ADAM *has become the* HOME OFFICE REPRESENTATIVE.

HOME OFFICE REPRESENTATIVE. Did you report your alleged sexual assault to the Egyptian police, Miss Kashmiry?

GLASGOW ADAM. Alleged? I...

HOME OFFICE REPRESENTATIVE. Did you report your attack to the Egyptian police?

GLASGOW ADAM *gives a shake of the head.*

So you did not feel significantly threatened?

GLASGOW ADAM. I did.

HOME OFFICE REPRESENTATIVE. Why then did you not seek redress or protection?

GLASGOW ADAM. I, I don't understand the question. From whom could I seek protection?

HOME OFFICE REPRESENTATIVE. The police, of course.

GLASGOW ADAM. If I tell the police that a person on the street has hurt me, they hurt me twice as bad. I tell them I was sexually assaulted by a man. Three police assault me. Redress? Protection? There is none.

HOME OFFICE REPRESENTATIVE. So to clarify, Miss Kashmiry, there is no formal record of your attack?

Nothing to prove it ever happened at all.

Faced with the impossible Catch-22 logic, GLASGOW ADAM *steps out of the memory.*

GLASGOW ADAM. I'm stuck in a palindrome. Backwards, forwards, everywhere my fate is the same. Madam I'm Adam.

Images from the Arab world (2011 as the Arab Spring gathers momentum) flicker on to the screens.

EGYPTIAN ADAM. What is happening at home?

GLASGOW ADAM. This room is my brain.

EGYPTIAN ADAM. People are protesting. Our brothers and sisters are screaming for change.

GLASGOW ADAM. I am trapped inside my brain.

EGYPTIAN ADAM. Look! How can this be happening?

GLASGOW ADAM *looks for the first time.*

GLASGOW ADAM. The internet.

This thought prompts GLASGOW ADAM*'s renewed preoccupation with the internet, the laptop is opened again.*

EGYPTIAN ADAM. This has nothing to do with –

GLASGOW ADAM. People are daring to ask things online that they wouldn't ask aloud. They are meeting people who are changing them, helping each other to act. Just like I did.

EGYPTIAN ADAM. It's bubbling over like a volcano. Revolution everywhere. Tunisia, Libya, Yemen, Bahrain.

GLASGOW ADAM. I will find it in this room. The proof that I am a man.

EGYPTIAN ADAM. And in Egypt, Mubarak is overthrown.

GLASGOW ADAM. It's possible to buy testosterone online!

EGYPTIAN ADAM. We have our first democratically elected leader in sixty years! Mama will be so happy. I should be there.

GLASGOW ADAM. Without a bank card, it's almost impossible but I've found one site where you can pay by Western Union. It costs… forty-two pounds.

EGYPTIAN ADAM. Seven pounds more than I have each week to live on?

GLASGOW ADAM. I don't need food.

Days pass. We're into the 300s. The ADAMS *pace and prowl.* GLASGOW ADAM *returns frequently to the internet, which angers* EGYPTIAN ADAM *who slams the laptop shut and thrusts a toilet roll in* GLASGOW ADAM*'s face.*

EGYPTIAN ADAM. It's nearly finished…

GLASGOW ADAM. You use too much. One sheet. One sheet per visit.

EGYPTIAN ADAM. The toothpaste's run out.

GLASGOW ADAM. Brush without it.

EGYPTIAN ADAM. What about my period? I have no sanitary towels.

GLASGOW ADAM (*rhetorical*). Has it started?

EGYPTIAN ADAM. Not *yet*.

GLASGOW ADAM. So stop giving me problems!

EGYPTIAN ADAM. I'm hungry.

GLASGOW ADAM. *I'm* hungry!

EGYPTIAN ADAM. I will eat the last Weetabix.

GLASGOW ADAM. No! Save it.

EGYPTIAN ADAM. I can feel my bones jutting out through my skin.

GLASGOW ADAM *opens the laptop again.*

GLASGOW ADAM. This room is my brain. I will find the answers in this room.

EGYPTIAN ADAM. I am tired of being always in my brain. These 'friends' who help me on the internet? Can I touch them? At home, people are holding each other by the hand in solidarity. The internet did not start the revolution. Bouazizi did.

GLASGOW ADAM. The street vendor?

EGYPTIAN ADAM. His wheelbarrow of produce is confiscated again by corrupt police officials who he has no money to bribe. He appeals to them. He is hungry, desperate.

GLASGOW ADAM. My appeal! Months I've waited to hear and nothing. And now? Have they granted me asylum?

EGYPTIAN ADAM. They are deaf to him. He is trapped.

GLASGOW ADAM. I have been rejected. Again.

EGYPTIAN ADAM. They hold all the power.

GLASGOW ADAM. I am trapped.

EGYPTIAN ADAM. All his choices stolen from him, Bouazizi – a simple man – says 'Enough!'

He pours gasoline over himself and sets fire to his body. And starts a fire in the hearts of the entire Arab world.

GLASGOW ADAM. I feel like the climber in the film. Stuck for a hundred and twenty-seven hours between a boulder and the wall of a canyon.

EGYPTIAN ADAM. What film? I'm talking about revolution!

GLASGOW ADAM. The one I saw an advert for. The one I would see if I had any money.

EGYPTIAN ADAM. Forget films. Start a fire.

GLASGOW ADAM. How?

EGYPTIAN ADAM *can't answer this.*

Days pass. The ADAMS *pace and prowl.* EGYPTIAN ADAM *secretly sneaks the last Weetabix.* GLASGOW ADAM *sees and attacks. They grapple on the floor.*

Give it to me. That's mine.

EGYPTIAN ADAM. I'm hungry!

GLASGOW ADAM. I want it. Give it to me now.

GLASGOW ADAM *dominates* EGYPTIAN ADAM, *gets the Weetabix, nurses it for a moment, then has a moment of realisation. Calm again,* GLASGOW ADAM *laughs.*

I'm Gollum!

Laughs some more.

Or was he called Sméagol? I'm losing my fucking mind.

EGYPTIAN ADAM. Exile wasn't the only punishment in Ancient Egypt.

GLASGOW ADAM. This room is my brain. I kick the bed and my head throbs here.

EGYPTIAN ADAM. They would force a sinner to change their
   birth name and so part them for ever from their soul.

GLASGOW ADAM. I punch the wall and, here, I feel the ache
   of it.

   EGYPTIAN ADAM *begin to hyperventilate*.

EGYPTIAN ADAM. I can't breathe.

GLASGOW ADAM. I smash the mirror and feel a sharp pain
   behind my eye.

EGYPTIAN ADAM. I can't breathe.

   I need an ambulance. I cannot breathe. Am I dying?

GP (GLASGOW ADAM). Palpitations, hyperventilation,
   nausea, dizziness. It's another panic attack, Miss Kashmiry.
   You can't die from a panic attack. Did you try the breathing
   exercises?

EGYPTIAN ADAM (*still hyperventilating*). But this came from
   nowhere. I wasn't anxious, I wasn't upset. I was walking
   from the TV to the toilet. And suddenly, no breath at all.

GP. What were you watching?

EGYPTIAN ADAM. Channel 5. My TV only has Channel 5.

GP. That explains it then.

EGYPTIAN ADAM. I don't understand… oh, it's a joke,
   you're joking. Yes, Channel 5 is a very bad channel.

   The GP *is gone.* GLASGOW ADAM *ceremoniously presents
   a package.*

GLASGOW ADAM. It's here. The testosterone is here.

EGYPTIAN ADAM. And a syringe?

   GLASGOW ADAM *nods. They both expose their thighs.*

GLASGOW ADAM. The pharmacy would only give me this
   one for insulin. It's too small. It should be long and fat…

EGYPTIAN ADAM *sizes it up, warily.*

EGYPTIAN ADAM. A small needle is fine.

GLASGOW ADAM. The testosterone needs to reach the muscle. Injecting into the fat can really fuck you up. Give you an abscess, a fever...

It'll be okay though. Just need to avoid any blood vessels and hope for the best.

EGYPTIAN ADAM. How do I do it?

GLASGOW ADAM. Trust the brain. The primary motor cortex will send an electrical signal down the spinal cord to the muscles in the arm. And then... stab.

Both ADAMS *are primed. They stab the needles into their leg. Testosterone courses into their body. It is agony.* EGYPTIAN ADAM *begins to deteriorate from this moment on. It is a slow death.*

EGYPTIAN ADAM. It hurts. It really hurts.

GLASGOW ADAM. But not as much as slicing your own arm off with a pocket knife.

EGYPTIAN ADAM. What?

GLASGOW ADAM. The film about the climber trapped in a canyon. I looked up the ending.

EGYPTIAN ADAM. My leg feels dead. Like actually dead.

GLASGOW ADAM. My leg is black and swollen.

EGYPTIAN ADAM. This room is not straight. It is tipping left and right.

GLASGOW ADAM. My head is burning.

EGYPTIAN ADAM. Left.

GLASGOW ADAM. I'm on fire. I'm ice.

EGYPTIAN ADAM. And right.

GLASGOW ADAM. It's the testosterone. Oily and thick, seeping through the fat in my leg. It feels like I have been poisoned.

EGYPTIAN ADAM. Something is wrong in Egypt. Democracy is slipping away. Morsi has granted himself unlimited powers.

GLASGOW ADAM (*to the imagined interpreter after the Home Office interview*). Why are you laughing? You are here to translate my words to the Home Office interviewer. Not to laugh with him.

EGYPTIAN ADAM. Egypt has itself a new tyrant. The revolution has failed.

GLASGOW ADAM *as* TRANSLATOR *laughs longer than feels comfortable. Stops, then laughs again. Stops.*

TRANSLATOR. This is one of the strangest interviews I've ever done.

EGYPTIAN ADAM. I'm going to be sick.

EGYPTIAN ADAM *rushes away to vomit.*

GLASGOW ADAM. I have evidence, documents to prove. This report from a psychiatrist see 'in my professional opinion' – 'insistent, persistent and consistent' – that's me.

Here – this is a photograph of me at my all-girl school. See amongst all those smiling girls' faces, there short hair, skinny boy with a look of blackness on my face, forced to sit in a girl's uniform. Does that help? What else can I give you?

EGYPTIAN ADAM *throws a slimy brain on the floor.*

EGYPTIAN ADAM. Show them that.

GLASGOW ADAM. My brain! Does it look like a man's brain? Does it have the same volume and density of neurons as a man's? Does it prove it?

Days pass. The ADAMS *pace and prowl.*

It's time for another injection.

EGYPTIAN ADAM. I'm hungry.

GLASGOW ADAM. The testosterone will be our meal.

EGYPTIAN ADAM. My leg still hurts. The fever has only just calmed.

GLASGOW ADAM. It's time.

EGYPTIAN ADAM. It's like being bitten by a snake.

They expose their legs, heavy and bruised, agony to touch.

My hand won't move.

GLASGOW ADAM. The brain will send a signal.

EGYPTIAN ADAM. My body and brain aren't friends.

GLASGOW ADAM. Exactly.

They stab the needle again. Agony. Pacing becomes crawling. Fever. Madness.

What is the word – same word for two opposites? What is that word?

EGYPTIAN ADAM. We need to let the bird out of the cage? The green bird keeps bumping against the walls.

GLASGOW ADAM. What bird?

EGYPTIAN ADAM. It is Ba. It's my soul.

GLASGOW ADAM (*remembering*). Ba and Ka. The two parts of the soul.

EGYPTIAN ADAM. Separated from their body, their name, their shadow, they can be lost for ever.

GLASGOW ADAM. BAKA. KABA. Which is which?

EGYPTIAN ADAM. B is for bird. Ba is a human-headed bird.

GLASGOW ADAM. And K is for crazy? So Ka is what? A bird-headed human?

EGYPTIAN ADAM. The life force.

MENTAL-HEALTH NURSE (EGYPTIAN ADAM). Why did the GP give you our number, Adam?

GLASGOW ADAM. She thinks I want to commit suicide.

MENTAL-HEALTH NURSE. Do you?

GLASGOW ADAM. Can any person not think of suicide in this Glasgow weather?

There's a word I can't remember. It is an English word for two things that are opposites – do you know it?

MENTAL-HEALTH NURSE. I don't think so.

GLASGOW ADAM. Bound. I am bound somewhere, like Frodo heading for Mordor. But also I am bound. Tied up. Trapped.

MENTAL-HEALTH NURSE. How old are you, Adam?

GLASGOW ADAM. I am nineteen. But I feel ninety. Who are you? Did I let you in? Why are you here in my brain?

EGYPTIAN ADAM. Can you see the bird? I've lost it.

GLASGOW ADAM. It's time for the next injection.

EGYPTIAN ADAM. It's killing me.

GLASGOW ADAM. I know.

EGYPTIAN ADAM. There's a better way. To prove to them.

GLASGOW ADAM (*holding the needle*). This is the way.

EGYPTIAN ADAM. I'll cut them off. These – (*Gestures to their breasts.*) tumours. I'll take the blade to them. My primary motor cortex will send its signal and the blade will cut into the flesh.

GLASGOW ADAM. No need for blood.

EGYPTIAN ADAM. The revolution is not dead. Morsi is deposed. Because my brothers and sisters dare to pick up the knife.

EGYPTIAN ADAM *picks up the knife and slices through the chest binding, giving ribs space to breathe at last. Then folds a towel and places it nearby on the floor.*

Nothing changes without spilling blood.

EGYPTIAN ADAM *dials 999 on phone*.

Ambulance please. Adam. Yes. It's for me. I am about to take a knife to my chest. I'm going to cut them off. Come quickly please.

EGYPTIAN ADAM *puts down the phone and puts blade to breast*.

An Arabic lament overlaid with the sound of the emergency services.

'Miss, miss, are you still on the line. Miss…'

The knife is pressed into the breast, the lament surges and then silence.

Suspended in a dark void, out of time and space, GLASGOW ADAM *speaks*.

GLASGOW ADAM. The last American film I saw in Egypt was called Sunshine. Space in this film feels very real. When the astronauts throw themselves from one spaceship to another, it's fast and physical and within seconds they are back in gravity, the weight of the spacesuit, the pain of the body.

One of them doesn't make the jump. With no cord to anchor him, he floats away into the endless blackness. I envy that guy. The others have to keep their eyes on the sun, keep fighting for life but he is free.

I am a human-headed bird watching from a dark corner of the room.

My green-feathered wings are beating against the grey walls, against the painted-shut window. I watch my woman's body try to cut away flesh. Is that me? With testosterone coursing through it, the body I was born with has… died. The name I was born with has died. I am half a soul. I have no anchor. Without Ka – the spark, the life force, Ba is lost.

My ancestors feared this above all else. To be adrift. But a lost bird is better than a caged one. I have no need of that body and

I can feel myself turning away from the sun, towards endless blackness...

We are back in the room. EGYPTIAN ADAM *is gone.*
GLASGOW ADAM, *lifeless, is where* EGYPTIAN ADAM
held the knife moments before. Suddenly, movement –
GLASGOW ADAM *stabs the needle of testosterone into
thigh. It's like a shot of adrenaline and* GLASGOW ADAM
gasps. Alive. A door is opened. Light floods into the room.

Let There Be Light

GLASGOW ADAM. I wish I remembered what those words
were called that are two opposite things. Saleem. The snake
bite... cured me! I never have another period.

Puberty hits for the second time. Where the oestrogen
softened and rounded me, the testosterone thickens and
strengthens me. My body fat redistributes away from my
hips and legs to my internal organs and abdomen. My body
mass increases. My feet grow.

GLASGOW ADAM *kicks off both shoes and steps into
another pair and even another. Each time, growing in
stature.*

This is the opposite of the princess in the fairytale with the
glass slipper that fits. For my happy ending, all the shoes
need to stop fitting.

Looking at both feet and laughing, GLASGOW ADAM *lifts
them up to show the audience.*

I have hobbit feet!

My voice deepens. Hair is growing all over my body and
I love it. Thick black hairs claiming my flesh.

I wonder if Sauron has been in my brain with me. His big
eye watching me.

Because it's only now, now that I have ripped myself into manhood, that I receive notification that I have been granted asylum. I have proved myself a man. Now nurses will administer the testosterone without the pain and fever.

A surgeon will sculpt my chest without need for blood-soaked towel or ambulance. A team of doctors will take blood vessels from my arm, grafts from my legs and buttocks and shape me a fine manly cock.

I can exist in the world at last. Leave this room behind. This room in which I have lived for six hundred desperate days. I turn my back on it and step out into the watery Glasgow sun.

GLASGOW ADAM *steps out of the flat and into the world. He is bathed in beautiful coloured light.*

I am in Maryhill Burgh Hall looking up at stained-glass windows. A little plaque tells me they are called Adam's Stained-Glass Panels. Of course! I own the whole world now.

The windows show men in their working clothes. It says that these pictures are unique because usually the workers would be depicted as angels but here they are allowed to be themselves. The light shines through these men onto my face with its black stubble. Their light casting my shadow. The same shadow I was born with in Egypt in 1992, though my body and name are different. It is an angel's blessing from these working men for me – allowed to be my whole self at last.

A wall of leaflets behind me is also bathed in their light. One in particular from the Scottish Refugee Council inviting refugees and Scots to participate in an event called Here We Stay. A month ago, I wouldn't have even seen it but today, I am newborn and I think. Why not?

I am backstage in the Citizen's Theatre. There are splats of paint on the black floor and it smells musty and full of promise. In an hour I am supposed to stand up in front of an audience and tell them my story. But I can't do it. Instead, I'm here, hiding in a room full of costumes, racks bending under the weight of so many clothes. It reminds me of the shop I worked in back home. But there are more choices here, more fabrics and colours. Here are clothes from different times and places. I imagine what it would be like to dress as an Edwardian gentleman or a Highland chief. And I can't shake the feeling that either would feel less like a 'costume' than the girls' clothes Mama dressed me in all those years ago.

Mama.

My phone is out of my bag, FaceTime opened and dialled, before I am conscious of what I am doing.

GLASGOW ADAM *holds out his phone to FaceTime* MARYAM.

Before I Formed You in the Womb I Knew You

On the screen behind we see the 'real' MARYAM (an Arabic woman in her fifties).

MARYAM. Hello.

GLASGOW ADAM. Mama.

MARYAM. Princess?

GLASGOW ADAM *doesn't know how to answer.*

The image is a little… is it you?

GLASGOW ADAM. It's me.

MARYAM. You have a beard.

GLASGOW ADAM. I do.

This is impossible for MARYAM to process. She covers with nervous babble.

MARYAM. I'm glad you called because it gave me an excuse to hang up on your auntie. Forty minutes she has been bragging about her grandson, how well he reads now, how good he is at counting, she would invite me to admire the smell of his shit if she thought she could get away with it. And I can't see –

GLASGOW ADAM. Mama...

MARYAM. – what all the fuss is about because, to me, he seems very stupid and he is always picking his nose.

GLASGOW ADAM. No! I don't want these words.

An echo of MARYAM*'s earlier words to* ADAM, MARYAM *is silenced.*

I am supposed to go on stage, Mama. I am supposed to tell an audience of this crazy journey I've been on from Egypt to Glasgow, from girl to man.

A moment for her to receive this.

And I don't think I can do it until I have told it to you.

I am a man now, Mama. And my name is Adam.

MARYAM. What... what have you done to your body? What can you have...? I gave birth to that body, I bathed it, massaged it with oils, I kissed it, I loved it. It's my body as much as yours.

GLASGOW ADAM. I am sorry, Mama. I'm sorry I found it so hard to be happy. I'm sorry I alienated Baba and my cousin, I'm sorry I had to leave Egypt with no word. But I am not sorry about what I have done to my body. It is mine and not yours.

MARYAM. You are scarred.

GLASGOW ADAM. You used to say, a beautiful thing is not perfect.

MARYAM. My mother said it. I can hear her voice still. She would weep to know what you are.

GLASGOW ADAM. Do you remember our contract? Say it for me please.

MARYAM. I promise to be kind.
I promise not to hurt others.
I promise always to tell the truth.

GLASGOW ADAM. I never broke that contract, Mama. Can you say the same?

A moment. This lands for MARYAM.

I need to go. I'm on soon. I need something from you. I wouldn't ask if it wasn't... I need you to tell me you love me.

MARYAM. I do.

GLASGOW ADAM. I need you to tell it to me, your son. Not your princess, not ana bahibbik.

Can you do that? We have so much ahead of us if you can.

MARYAM. And if I can't?

GLASGOW ADAM *doesn't answer. There is no future for them if she can't. This causes them both pain.* GLASGOW ADAM *realises she can't.*

GLASGOW ADAM. Okay.

I must go.

MARYAM. I won't wish you luck for the performance.

GLASGOW ADAM. No?

MARYAM. Because you won't need it. Just tell the truth. Adam.

Ana bahibbak.

The screens flicker off.

GLASGOW ADAM *is overjoyed. He walks to the front of the stage.*

GLASGOW ADAM. I am here. I can see all these faces looking up at me. Sweat is forming on my top lip. I feel my heart beating hard here. Boom. Boom. Boom. I am alive.

Eyes are meeting mine and these eyes tell me they don't hate me, they understand. They remind me of the people who helped me when I first typed my question into the computer. Is it possible for the soul of a man to be trapped in the body of a woman? The answer is yes. When I finish people come up to me, shake my hand, hi-fives and hugs. It's a fucking buzz. This is better than getting home to the Shire.

Adam was Made a Living Soul

TONI *steps out from the audience. We have not met her before.*

TONI. Hi. That was fantastic.

GLASGOW ADAM. Oh, thank you. I'm glad you liked it.

TONI. I'm Toni…

Have you done anything like this before?

GLASGOW ADAM. No, I. This is new.

TONI. You were really relaxed.

GLASGOW ADAM. I was shitting myself.

TONI. You looked like you were enjoying it.

GLASGOW ADAM. I was! It was both at once. There's a term for words that are two things at once, opposites. Finished is one of them. I have finished, completed something which is good. Or I'm finished. Destroyed. Which is bad.

TONI. Contranym.

GLASGOW ADAM. What?

TONI. A word that is two opposite things. Contranym.

GLASGOW ADAM. That's it. That's the word. Contranym!

What follows is a seduction.

TONI. To seed. To remove seeds but also to plant them.

GLASGOW ADAM. To wind up – to finish something or to start it.

TONI. Temper – to strengthen or to soften.

An awkward pause.

GLASGOW ADAM. Are you going to stay behind for a drink? I mean I think there's going to be a group of us so… but if you've got somewhere you need to be –

TONI (*a bit too keen*). No! I don't need to be anywhere. That's cool I can. Yeah.

TONI *is embarrassed.*

I just thought of another one. Transparent –

GLASGOW ADAM. Like invisible or –

TONI (*said almost like a confession of her crush*). Or obvious.

GLASGOW ADAM *smiles, then takes* TONI*'s hand, very awkward and very shy. This turns into something of a dance.* TONI *touches* ADAM*'s body. In an echo of the scene with* AMIRA, *she touches* ADAM*'s chest.* GLASGOW ADAM *tenses up and looks as if he will stop her, then he relaxes and lets her. They continue their sort of dance, intimate and tender.*

The global choir begins. The voices that helped ADAM *on his journey. They are more harmonious now.* MARYAM *joins their number, her Arabic melody 'Ana bahibbak' complementing the rich and soaring harmonies until… blackout.*

'A great published script makes you understand what the play is, at its heart' *Slate Magazine*

Enjoyed this book? Choose from hundreds more classic and contemporary plays from Nick Hern Books, the UK's leading independent theatre publisher.

Our full range is available to browse online now, including:

Award-winning plays from leading contemporary dramatists, including *King Charles III* by Mike Bartlett, *Anne Boleyn* by Howard Brenton, *Jerusalem* by Jez Butterworth, *A Breakfast of Eels* by Robert Holman, *Chimerica* by Lucy Kirkwood, *The Night Alive* by Conor McPherson, *The James Plays* by Rona Munro, *Nell Gwynn* by Jessica Swale, and many more…

Ground-breaking drama from the most exciting up-and-coming playwrights, including Vivienne Franzmann, James Fritz, Ella Hickson, Anna Jordan, Jack Thorne, Phoebe Waller-Bridge, Tom Wells, and many more…

Twentieth-century classics, including *Cloud Nine* by Caryl Churchill, *Death and the Maiden* by Ariel Dorfman, *Pentecost* by David Edgar, *Angels in America* by Tony Kushner, *Long Day's Journey into Night* by Eugene O'Neill, *The Deep Blue Sea* by Terence Rattigan, *Machinal* by Sophie Treadwell, and many more…

Timeless masterpieces from playwrights throughout the ages, including Anton Chekhov, Euripides, Henrik Ibsen, Federico García Lorca, Christopher Marlowe, Molière, William Shakespeare, Richard Brinsley Sheridan, Oscar Wilde, and many more…

Every playscript is a world waiting to be explored. Find yours at **www.nickhernbooks.co.uk** – you'll receive a 20% discount, plus free UK postage & packaging for orders over £30.

'Publishing plays gives permanent form to an evanescent art, and allows many more people to have some kind of experience of a play than could ever see it in the theatre' *Nick Hern, publisher*

www.nickhernbooks.co.uk

www.nickhernbooks.co.uk

 facebook.com/nickhernbooks

 twitter.com/nickhernbooks